Reset &

Reboot

Regaining
Mindfulness

Esmeralda Baez

ELITE VISION MEDIA
PUBLISHING

Reset and Reboot
Regaining Mindfulness
© 2022 by Esmeralda Baez

ISBN-13:
979-8-218-03277-7- Paperback
979-8-218-03278-4- Hardcover
Library of Congress Control Number: 2022912848

Printed in the United States of America.

ELITE VISION MEDIA PUBLISHING
New York, NY

Table of Contents

A Dedication to You

When I decided to begin the journey of writing my story and sharing my truth, my editor asked me who my avatar was. At first, I did not understand, and then she explained that when she works with authors, she asks them who we see holding the book in their hands? Who do we see in our hearts reading what we are about to release?

Within seconds, I thought of the perfectly imperfect version of ourselves. I thought about the many times I felt broken, confused, tired, anxious, full of self-doubts and regrets, alone, and forsaken. I remembered the times when I needed to be shaken and reminded that I was placed on this earth with a purpose and that I was not a mistake. I remembered when I needed to find inspiration to believe, once again, that I didn't have to be afraid to be who I am. So, when I thought about my avatar, I thought about *you*. I saw myself telling *you* to dare to dream, explore, love, and be different because we need more souls like yours.

I felt the need to share my truth with you. I know how difficult it is to swim upstream going against all odds. I am a Latin woman, considered an immigrant and minority, self-made entrepreneur, who has had to overcome many challenges and stigmas to be where I am today.

This is not an ordinary book to motivate you. These pages are designed to reach deep into your soul and plant a seed of worth and purpose so you can begin to live your life the way it was intended and created for you.

You were created for greatness, not sorrow. You deserve to be fully loved, not partially. I do not want to motivate you; I want you to be mentally transformed so you can flourish in any soil in which you are planted. Tomorrow is not guaranteed, but if you can let go of your past, the negativity, and stop worrying about the future, you will have the opportunity to be present in the day you have today and make each moment count.

It took a near-death experience and a cerebrovascular disease to stop me in my tracks and make me appreciate the little things in life that make it worth living.

As you start the journey within these pages, my deepest desire is that you find the hidden treasures designed to breathe life back into your lungs and make you fall in love again with yourself, the universe, and your purpose. All of your dreams and goals are coming your way. Trust the process and timing of your life. Do not, for one second, lose hope.

Esmeralda Baez

SKIN-DEEP

"To love who you are, you cannot hate the experiences that shaped you. Make the decision to live more from intention than from habit. The goal is to grow so strong on the inside that nothing on the outside can affect your inner wellness without your permission."

I believe that at some point, we all have had the desire to go back into the past and change an event, outcome, experience, or decision that we regret ever happened. But the reality is that no matter how hard, complicated, or negative a past event was, it's exactly that: your past! Everything you have lived has played a role in who you are today and who you can be tomorrow. Your past doesn't define you; it just shows where you came from and how much you have progressed.

There was a moment in my life when the unexpected event of a brain aneurysm occurred, and in all honesty, it stirred my spirit. I didn't have much information on what it was or how it would affect my life. It was a scary moment, but I was too eager to succeed in life to let that season hold me back. Being diagnosed forced me to reflect on many things in my life, but most importantly, it motivated me to fight and improve so that I could continue living. This time I understood what truly mattered and what I wanted to accomplish following this event.

I had been dealt with a card I was not expecting, so I had one of two choices to make: I could roll up into a ball and dwell in this situation, or I could go skin-deep into it and use it to change my life and inspire others. I chose to use it to inspire others through my social media platforms and now this book so that men and women can see the importance of daily practicing healthy habits to attain better physical and mental health outcomes. Instead of just surviving, I desire for people to thrive. Too many people just exist but do not live life to the fullest potential. Wellness is a lifestyle of perfect harmony with physical and mental health.

Unfortunately, our culture downplays mental health as if it isn't the most important thing we should worry about. Physical problems are regularly easy to notice, but mental health issues can take you by surprise. This is a very big issue, especially in the Latin community.

Social media influencers have played a big part in the physical aspect of how people think they should look or dress, but how many influencers do you see motivating others to do their annual checkups? How many socialites do you hear that use their platforms to motivate others to make time for mental health wellness checkups? Unfortunately, there are not enough.

The biggest battlefield we have is in our minds and through our emotions. There is a saying that God uses the heart, but the devil uses emotions.

> **"** If your mind and emotions are in the dark, everything else malfunctions.

The brain is the most beautiful but complex organ in our bodies and sometimes the most dangerous one we have.

Our emotions and thought processes are all connected. Emotions generate thoughts, and thoughts generate actions. If those thoughts are out of balance or not in line with your well-being, your actions, or lack of actions, can take you down a path of self-destruction. Living a healthy lifestyle is not just a matter of eating healthy, exercising, drinking enough water, and so on, but it's also having a healthy mindset, emotional intelligence, and achieving a spiritual balance.

Having experimented unexpected situations brought me to this moment. I want to discuss with you six crucial areas of your life that if maintained in harmony, they can result in robust mindfulness and a perfect balance that will evolve into peace, resilience, and stability. The best version of yourself is just a decision away. There is no better investment and nothing more valuable than wanting to reach your best self.

This book is a tool designed to take you on a self-discovery path with the purpose to rest and reboot the way you think, feel, and view your past, current, and future circumstances. There are moments where you will primarily need to go through it alone, and in others, there is a benefit to making this voyage accompanied with people who add value to your life.

Even though the journey toward self-discovery and awareness is typically initiated alone, I believe people don't always need time alone to figure it out. Humans need human interaction. Having a friend, partner, or mentor with whom to live this adventure can be fun too. We all need love and affection, but at the same time, we also need to embrace solitude. It's finding that middle ground and perfect equilibrium that will make this a beautiful experience.

I want you to make space today for self-reflection and self-care. Always remember to take time out of your day to check in with *you*. Remind yourself that you are worthy of everlasting happiness, and you are beautiful.

No one is *you*! I can almost guarantee that in the last few years, you have encountered many people imposing views on the way you should live, look, or the way you should perceive life; all I can say is close to your ears and mind to them. I'm not sure exactly what you might be going through emotionally at this time; however, just know that no one has the right to choose what makes you feel good about yourself; *only you can*!

Everyone is entitled to make their own choices, but please be careful who you allow in your inner circle because they can either break or make you! Be wise enough to choose who has an effect in your life.

The universe is a beautiful place with all sorts of flavors and styles, and the mind's natural inclination is to judge, but you can neglect that by inverting bad thoughts into good ones. This is why I truly believe that when we practice love, acceptance, and forgiveness, we truly live with essence. Compassion and love will eventually set you *free.* Condemnation, shame, and blame will only imprison you. So, stop beating yourself up over things you can't control.

We all have a story, and what's on the outside is merely a painting on a canvas! My question to you is: how do your insides look? The only thing you should strive for is fulfillment and inner peace; the only way you can achieve that is by being happy with what you see in the mirror every day. Keep in mind that what other people may think of you is *not* your business. Don't let negativity dictate your worth. I hope you tell yourself today that you're worthy of it all, and the only thing you should desire to adjust are things within yourself.

We are all works in progress, and you will be good as long as you are willing to do the work. Toughen up, hold your head high, and trust God's timing. Remember that your current reality isn't necessarily your truth but a temporary season.

I challenge you to document your process as you take this voyage. Writing has healing power. It will be a very interesting result when you go back and compare the notes of the person who started and the person you will be tomorrow. Keep a journal of your emotions and do not be afraid to be brutally honest with yourself in the process. Today I am inspiring you so that tomorrow you can pay it forward.

As I stated in the opening of this chapter: "To love who you are, you cannot hate the experiences that shaped you. Make the decision to live more from intention than from habit. The goal is to grow so strong on the inside that nothing on the outside can affect your inner wellness without your permission." I am very excited to live this experience with you. The next six chapters will take you through a true introspection that will only result in a better version of yourself. If you are up to the challenge, flip the page, and let's begin the journey.

SORROW

"When I fully understood that I don't have the power to change things that already happened and there was no value in wishing things were different, that was the day I started living to my fullest potential."

Sorrow, a six-letter word defined as a feeling of deep distress caused by loss, disappointment, or other misfortune suffered by oneself or others; that is the definition you will find if you look up this word as described on the Merriam-Webster dictionary. How many of us can honestly say we know firsthand what that feels like? How many can confess to feeling those exact emotions when life has happened and the rug has been pulled down from under our feet? What the dictionary cannot tell you are the side effects that dwelling in this feeling can bring to your life.

This is the first area I wish for you to take a close look at in your journey to resetting your brain and gaining mindfulness: your sorrows. The truth is that loss, disappointment, heartbreak, misfortune, and sickness, among many other things, truly do provoke great pain and sadness. It can be very dark and confusing. Many people, even you, have stopped living even though they are alive because of past events and miseries. Unexpected turnouts can leave you feeling empty and feeling hopeless. Nevertheless, there can be true beauty and growth within pain and sorrow.

Answer the following questions: how have you viewed your hardships in the past? Have you settled for less because you have felt unworthy of more? Did you stop chasing your dreams because you felt nothing goes your way? Have you been afraid to try again because of the fear of getting hurt? Do you currently feel you move five steps forward and then fall ten steps back? Lastly, have you ever celebrated a loss? That is right, you read correctly. Have you ever celebrated and been thankful for your losses and hardships?

This last question will surprise you. We have grown up believing that losses are negative things and failures are reflections of defeat. In reality, it is completely the opposite. Every failure, loss, and event that has resulted in defeat has only placed you closer to success, a win or gain.

Think about it for one minute. When you read or hear the testimonies of different influencers, famous people, and successful businessmen and women, they all have one thing in common: they all went through many no's before getting their first yes. These people have turned their hardships into lessons that took them closer to their final goal. We can find examples everywhere we look.

In history, we learned that Thomas Alva Eddison made 1,000 unsuccessful attempts at inventing the light bulb before landing on the 1,001 that functioned. Oprah Winfrey was turned away for being "unfit" for television; Walt Disney was fired for not being creative enough, and Vera Wang did not succeed at her first choice of career. All these famous and rich people today experienced many losses and went through many sorrows, but they did not give up. You can find their stories and many more on any webpage on the internet.

Still today, there are hundreds of people trying to cure cancer, diabetes, and other illnesses, and they have not stopped because every failure leaves behind a great lesson. They now know what did not work and will be sure to not use the same method. The same applies to us. This is the hidden treasure behind the pain and beauty that is revealed once the situation rolls over: growth. Letting go and growth hurts, but the end result of a difficult process is the resilience that it brings along.

One of the most powerful and eye-opening experiences you can live is doing a recap of everything you have been through and realizing that you are stronger than you think. You have the ability to overcome any situation if you set your mind correctly. At the beginning of this chapter, I stated: "When I fully understood that I didn't have the power to change things that already happened and that there was no value in wishing things were different, that was the day I started living to my fullest potential."

No one can physically go to the past and change the outcome of things that have occurred, and no matter how hard we desire it, what resulted from past events can't change. Nevertheless, you do have the power and ability to change the way you view past events and the way you emotionally relate to them.

True power is having the ability to transform sorrows and negativity into positive energy that gives you the upper hand over your emotional stability. A simple example is when I began to replace my *"I'm sorry"* with *"Thank you."* For example, instead of saying, *"Sorry, I'm late,"* I will say, *"Thanks for waiting for me,"* or instead of saying, *"Sorry, I'm such a mess,"* I'll say, *"Thank you for loving and caring for me unconditionally."*

This exercise has not only shifted the way I think and feel about myself, but it has also improved my relationship with others. Now they receive my gratitude instead of negativity. Pain and hardships are part of life, and there is very little you can do to avoid things from happening, but what you do own are your thoughts, feelings, and emotions.

If you are documenting this journey, now is the time to look back and start writing and meditating on everything that you have overcome. What can you say about those experiences? What knowledge did you gain? Do you feel stronger today?

When I did this self-reflection, I discovered that everything I went through in life reflected my attitude, choices, and habits. Learning how to control and manage all of these variables positively impacted my life.

You can take back the control of your mental and emotional health. Your bad days are part of your life story, and you are the only narrator. I understand people who have survived trauma and have come out the other side furious and spitting blood and did not give up. I understand those who have survived trauma and ended up subdued, smaller, and less brave, as well as those who refuse to deal with their trauma who fuck, fight, and run. I understand those who are in the middle of dealing with their pain and cry on the floor one day and feel invincible the next.

Every person manages sorrows differently. There is not a one-size-fits-all remedy, but if you choose to make every pain a step, every tear a seed, and every defeat a learning lesson, you will have the power to see light in the darkness, flowers in the desert, and beauty in the displeasing.

A change of perspective can change the way you think, which, in turn, will change the way you make decisions. A failure is a failure if you did not learn anything from it. A loss is only a loss if you never received anything good from when you experienced it. I saw an anonymous quote from an unknown author that said: *"Don't be afraid to start over again; this time you're not starting from scratch, your starting from experience."* Let go of your past, enjoy your present, and have faith for the future. Use every experience that broke you in the past and create a beautiful mosaic of who you are today.

Take time every day to realize you are a survivor. It is probable that other people who have experienced similar situations you have overcome did not make it. But you are still here, reading this book, and making an effort to start living and not just existing.

There are so many extraordinary adventures waiting for you, but you have to stop dwelling in the past, and you must stop embracing pain and fear. You were not created to live in fear. You are the biggest and most beautiful creation upon the earth. I believe in you! Now, you must believe in yourself. Start doing the work and face head-on your current challenges.

I warned you that this book is not just a pep talk or was created with the intention to cheer you up. My greatest desire is that with all of the areas we will discuss, your spirit will shake, and you will revive the desire to reach your maximum potential so that you can start living under the purpose for which you were created.

Growth is beautiful, but so is gratitude. Do not be so focused on the next level that you forget to enjoy the present and how far you have come. This will be a beautiful healing process, and you can enjoy it if you truly open up to resetting and rebooting your mindset. Sometimes to move forward, advance, and reach the levels you have not been able to, you need to forget, erase, break habits and customs, and give yourself the opportunity to allow new knowledge and information to take you into a world you had not seen before. I want to remind you that no one is coming to your house to make your dreams come true. If you are not where you want to be in life, you must work every minute and snatch every opportunity that comes before you.

You are not your circumstances, you are not a victim, and you were not placed on this earth to make others happy while sacrificing your own wellness. You flipped the page to begin your journey toward a reset, and you are taking the steps to reboot your mind. You have gone to your past and have realized that someone else would have not been able to withstand what you overcame.

We are given one life and one opportunity. Do not spend another minute sitting on your failures or dwelling on what could have been. Get up, shake it off, and make the decisions you have to regain you inner peace. We cannot leave it all to faith. It will require intention and will to start seeing a difference.

Now that you have made a deep dive into your life and have transformed your hardships into stepping-stones, it is time to edit, cut, detox, and cast out anything and everything in your life that has held you back from being the person you were meant to be.

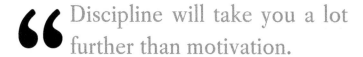 Discipline will take you a lot further than motivation.

Stay goal-oriented and hold yourself accountable. Create a plan, check your progress, make changes, and improve. It is time to clean the house!

DETOXIFICATION

"The best thing about your life is that it is constantly in a state of design. This means you have the power to redesign it at all times. Make moves, allow shifts, smile more, do more, do less, say no, say yes, and just remember that when it comes to your life, you are not just the artist but the masterpiece as well."

The most important decision you can make is to reset, reboot, and restart your life regardless of the age or stage you are currently in. It is never too late to start over and begin living the best version of yourself. Like in any regimen, when you begin, the suggestion is to start with a detox. Detox as described by the Oxford dictionary is a process or a period of time in which one abstains from or rids the body of toxic or unhealthy substances. That is exactly what you need to do so you can get rid of old habits, strongholds, and toxic people, things, and ideas. This detox has to be in all major areas of your life, and they are all enclosed in the perfect trilogy: body, mind, and spirit. The reason I mention the body, mind, and spirit is because this is the command center of our existence.

The body is the vessel in which our mind and spirit are carried. Our mind is what carries all of our thoughts, emotions, and everything that represents our character, personality, and human factors. The spirit is the balance between the two. This is the area that carries our will and helps center us when the body and mind are under deep stress. Each of these three areas needs a reset for us to start living and thinking differently and to begin to see different results. So, how do we start to detox those areas? Let us take a closer look into all three.

Let us begin with our bodies. Detoxing your body is not just a matter of eating healthier and drinking more water (which is a great start), but it is also taking care of the vessel that allows you to interact with others as well as being able to enjoy the world, nature, and your surroundings through your senses. You have to take control of your vessel and care for it, knowing you only get one.

Health starts with a smart choice of the food we eat, followed by the correct intake of water and liquids. Exercising is also a great practice to maintain your body in optimum conditions. There is a deeper connection between the brain and the gut than most people realize. Now, making sure to visit your physician once a year as a minimum to do the annual checkups is extremely important.

Sometimes we experience physical issues that are directly linked to our emotions. We might believe we are experiencing certain anxieties due to emotional imbalance when, in reality, there can be underlying health issues we have not considered or know about.

A few years ago, I started suffering from what I thought was severe anxiety. With the anxiety came palpitations, insomnia, panic attacks, and razing thoughts. After going to the psychiatrist, psychologists, and several therapies, the doctors confirmed I suffered from anxiety but also type A bipolar disorder. All of the symptoms I had come from an underlying condition of which I was not aware. That is why today I would like to use my voice to encourage you to keep medical appointments, get more sleep, eat right, stay fit, and recognize any abnormal signs or symptoms.

Do not be afraid to go to the doctor and ask questions, as scary as it may be, to find out if something's wrong with you. What may seem like devastating news can always open doors to a whole new world of possibilities.

I have come to realize the importance of living life and never complaining about the little things and just live life to the greatest potential. To enjoy that life we seek, the first step is to get our vessel into the correct state and cut away anything that goes against self-care and prevents a healthy lifestyle. You would not let your phone battery to completely die out; don't let it happen to you either. Self-care is a priority, not a luxury.

Next comes the mind, our biggest battlefield. This is the most critical area that we need to work on and the hardest to reboot because our emotions are tied into everything we do and everyone we allow in our lives. But in the mind is where we fight the toughest battles. Here, we need to start by learning how to reprogram every negative thought that turns into limitations in our heads.

Our thoughts are very powerful. They can hold you back or push you forward. So, you need to listen to your own voice and speak to yourself the truth you represent. Make a list of every dismissive, pessimistic, gloomy, and bad thought that has made a space for itself in your mind and counterattack it with your truth. For example: *I am ugly, I am not good enough, I don't have what it takes, I am too week, Nobody loves me, I am too old,* and so on. Anything and everything that has dwelled in your mind that goes against you, reprogram each of them with your truth: *Beauty is in the eye of the beholder, I am enough, I can achieve anything I work toward, I am strong, I am worthy, and I am my biggest fan and my truest love.*

66 You have the power to take to your heart what is generated from your mind.

Do not allow toxic thoughts to reside in your mind and convert into negative emotions. Go against them with the truth you know about yourself and let that truth be positive, reassuring, and constructive. Making sure to develop healthy sleeping habits will also be crucial in your process. Sleep is a process of restauration for the mind, body, and soul.

Once you cleanse your mind from negative thoughts, you will immediately see that reflected in your emotions. No one has power over you but yourself. Be careful not to be your biggest enemy but be your biggest fan.

Emotional intelligence is something we must work on every day. You cannot control what is around you, but like I have mentioned before, you *can* control how you react to everything. You decide if what others think about you is true or not. You decide what causes pain and what you take with you. You have the capability to turn every negative emotion into fuel to carry you over to your next stage. You are allowed to cry, hurt, rant, and be confused. It is ok not to be ok. What is not allowed is to remain in that stage. Life will continue with or without you. Pain and failure can be lessons or hurdles. The decision is yours.

People and environments are the next to be rebooted in your mind stage. Personally, this is the most complex area to detox because we create soul ties with people and environments. There are many emotional co-dependencies with people we know are not good for us, but we feel we cannot let go. The fact is that one person can change your life, and one person can also destroy it.

Be very selective in who you let in your life, especially when you are on the rise to success. Many people walk alone on their way up the ladder, but when others see them in a high position, they all want to accompany them. Be grateful for the ones who like you because of your strengths and virtues but who love you despite your flaws and weaknesses.

I always say I am not the person you want to hang out with if you are not ready to evolve because I will not sit there and listen to you complain about life and wear your pain like a trophy. I want people by my side who challenge me to be better every day.

The reality is we are all battling against something, and none of us are easy to be with. So when you meet someone willing to stay committed to understanding you and wants to grow with you, hang on to them tightly. Real is rare; remember that. The same goes for romantic relationships. The world is filled with good people, but not all good people are good for you.

If you are not growing and evolving next to the person you are with, or if you cry or hurt more than you laugh and enjoy in a relationship, it's time to move on. Remember, you only get one life. Make the best of it and enjoy it with people who challenge you to be better and celebrate every milestone you reach.

There are places, surroundings, and even workplaces that are not meant for you. If you are in a place that drags you, burdens you, or just creates negative energy for you, walk away. You are a unique piece of art. There is no other person in the world like you. You are one in billions. Find a place that can value that uniqueness and appreciate you, your talents, and your value. Do not shine less because your glitter bothers other people. You keep shining; they can always choose to wear sunglasses.

Finally, we reach the level of rebooting your spirit. We all need to connect to something. To some, they call it God, to others, nature or the universe. You need a safe place where you can disconnect and balance yourself every day.

I discovered the beauty and power of meditation. I enjoy the power of silence and how by releasing my thoughts, emotions, and the chaos that surrounds me, I can reboot my system and my entire mindset by attracting positive energy and thoughts into my mind. So whether it is prayer, meditation, fasting, or any other means, find time to slow down, breathe, and enjoy a moment with yourself.

You have to keep evolving and recreating yourself. Read, explore, and discover new things. Learning new things and expanding your mind will add versatility to your life. Go to retreats, travel, experience new cultures, try new foods, make new friends, and challenge yourself to step out of your comfort zone. You should not be who you were last week or in the past. Create new habits and constantly upgrade yourself in all ways and levels. Go above and beyond and flourish.

FLOURISH

"As a Latina immigrant, I didn't have the opportunity to sit at the table of big PR agencies, so I decided to build my own."

When you make a decision to reset your life, although people may be cut off and environments may change, the truth is that what becomes different is yourself and your perspective on all issues. Your world on the inside has changed, but many things around you might still be the same. If that is the case, now you have to flourish regardless of the soil you are planted in. The quote I used to start this chapter is 100 percent real.

In my heart, I always knew I was a people person, and I knew I had the capabilities to work in public relations despite any limitations the world wanted to label me. I thrive to make others shine. It is part of who I am. So, despite not having the opportunities to be received by these already-established big PR agencies, I decided to build my own and become my own brand.

That is exactly what I want you to start doing. You have done a deep dive introspection of yourself, you started to turn sorrows into lessons to move forward, and you cut out of your life everything that could hold you back.

The next natural step is to flourish. Flourish, by definition in the Oxford dictionary, means to grow or develop in a healthy or vigorous way, especially as the result of a particularly favorable environment. The world has not changed, but you definitely started to. This means you have to be your own cheerleader, your number-one fan, and you need to start going after your dreams. No one will do it for you. When you decide to reinvent yourself, you recharge your future. You do not have to settle for less. You can have it all. It is just a matter of creating the correct strategies that will take you there.

" Not everyone will agree with you or find you capable, and that is ok.

You just need to trust yourself and realize that you are enough. You have already allowed yourself to start changes, now you have to start taking chances. With risks come rewards, but if you do not step out of your comfort zone and try new things, you will never discover what your true potential is.

When you discover your passion and turn it into what you do every day, and it becomes a form of revenue, you will never feel you are working. You have converted your talents into provision. I am not saying it will be easy, but I am saying that it is possible to make a way for yourself. Sometimes we rely too much on external motivation, and that is never guaranteed. When motivation comes from within, it is a never-ending fountain of inspiration that does not depend on anyone else but you.

You are your own brand! No one else is responsible for your success; you are. If you are not satisfied with the results you see in your life today, change them. The best part about planting a seed is that in the process of something newly evolving, something old must die. You cannot move forward unless you let go of the past, and you won't be able to see different things unless you take risks, step out of your comfort zone, and tap into new possibilities. You can become someone else's inspiration when you begin to create new synergies and start building new relationships and when you are willing to leave the past behind.

You have to establish a dream and embrace it. When I came into the United States, I had a goal. I wanted to thrive. I finished my education, worked in hospitality for a few years, moved on to be a stylist for fashion brands and beauty pageants, among many other things, but never lost my north. I knew who I wanted to become, and I decided to go after it even if it meant creating it myself. Not everyone believed in me, but I believed in myself. Not everyone who was in my life supported my dream, but I was enough. I have never stopped believing that if I could dream it, it can come true.

I launched my PR Agency Elite Vision Media in 2019. The very next year, the pandemic hit. Yes, it was a challenge. Yes, there were days in which I had no idea what the outcome would be. But I knew that if I maintained my focus and cut out of my life all negative streams, I could overcome this uncertain situation as well.

What is your dream? How do you see yourself? Make a plan and stay focused. The soil will not always be favorable, the sun will not always come out to shine, and there will be days you will feel exhaustion and dryness, but if you work hard and surround yourself with visionaries and people who strive every day to be better than they were yesterday, you can achieve anything you set your mind to.

Start making your conversations about reaching goals, personal growth, and reaching the financial status you desire. You have to reach a point in your life where your only focus is to continue matching the frequency of the reality you want. Everything you have lived is a contribution to who you are today. It is not just the formal education you might or might not have achieved that makes you unique and successful; it is also the street smarts, hustler mentality, internal creativity, and your "know how to" that adds value that no degree can provide. So make sure that you are not selling yourself short. Do not establish limits on your possibilities.

As a business owner today, my goal is to not only be successful but also add value to others, as well as to be respected for my work ethic. That is why I am writing this book. I know you have the talent and ability to grow and flourish in any scenario you are willing to conquer. Stop letting your potential go to waste because you do not feel confident enough. People with half your talents are making serious waves while you are waiting to feel ready. The time to advance, move forward, evolve, and flourish is now. Own your power!

Make certain that you are spending your time on activities that are productive and take you in the direction of your goals. The person you will be in five years is based on the books you read and people you associate with today. Be very selective and intentional. You are your biggest and most valuable investment.

New goals do not deliver new results. New lifestyles do. A lifestyle is not an outcome; it is a process. For this reason, your energy should not go into chasing better results but on building better habits. If you believe you have already achieved your goals and stopped thriving, there is nothing left for you to work toward. You have to believe that there is a mountain so high that you will spend the rest of your life striving to reach the top of it. You need to continue to dream big, work hard, stay focused, and surround yourself with great people. Leave the rest to God. You will win! Not immediately, but definitely. Not because you are destined but because you are determined. So put on your seatbelt; it is going to be a bumpy ride. Some people may judge you for changing, but they are not really mad at you because you changed; they are mad at themselves for remaining the same! Please surround yourself with those who celebrate your growth.

ROLLER-COASTER

"Channel all of your energy on who you are becoming. What you want exists. So, don't stop until you get it!"

Life is an ongoing, moving, fun-filled adventure that will always keep you on your feet. It is a constant fluctuation of events that will occur regardless of your will. Life will continue to evolve; you decide if you progress and advance with it.

If I have learned anything, it's that every day is different, and nothing is final. Your journey toward a new form of thinking and a mindfulness transformation is the same. You must celebrate the highs, be aware of the lows, and enjoy the ride. This is crucial to understand because there will be days when everything seems to go flawless and in your favor, but there will be other times of true hardship. Since you can't predict the future, you can only make sure to have both scenarios in mind and rest assured to be in control of your emotions.

There is a famous Martin Luther King quote that says you cannot avoid birds from flying over your head, but you can keep them from building a nest on your hair. There will surely be good and bad days that you will not be able to control, but what you can control is how you react to them. Transformation is a constant roller-coaster. It doesn't look the same for every person, and it is definitely not a one-size-fits-all path. It will be different every day and in every aspect.

When you come to realize that within each day, you have the opportunity to live, there is a unique life experience waiting, and you become excited with what is to come. This is why it is important to not dwell in the past, no matter how beautiful or wonderful the experiences you lived. They are gone, and there is so much more waiting for you. The past can be a powerful stronghold; it can prevent you from enjoying your today and stop you from moving forward toward tomorrow.

> " I have learned only to visit the past to see how far I have come and appreciate where I am today.

Everybody has a story that can explain their today, but it is important that your past doesn't dominate your present. It doesn't matter how bad or good it was; it is not your current reality.

There are so many people who do not love today because they were hurt in the past. Others do not go after professional opportunities because they were rejected at some point in their lives or were told they didn't have what it takes. All past events have had an emotional impact in them, and many have kept themselves from believing they can achieve what their hearts desire. You have the power and authority to break with the past to optimize your present.

Regarding your present season, make sure you understand that the day you are currently living will never be repeated. It is literally one in a lifetime. Be sure to make the most of it. Some people fantasize with a perfect life (under what they believe is perfect) or a life full of permanent happiness. For some reason, they believe that a happy life is one in which there are no hardships, trials, or bad days. Living under this expectation will result in constant frustrations and deceptions because, as mentioned before, life is a moving organism perfectly balanced between good and bad. Truthfully, if you can find a happy moment in your day, every day, you are living a happy life. When you reach this realization and let go of the past, you can now focus on making the correct decisions today to see different results in the future.

Your present is the most valuable season you have. Tomorrow is not guaranteed, so stressing over things that have not occurred or happened only produces panic attacks and anxiety. Living in the past can detain you, but worrying about a future that is not guaranteed will prevent you from enjoying your today.

The world was created in seasons and timings: past, present, and future. We have four seasons in the year: summer, fall, winter, and spring. Each one is so unique and with distinctive characteristics of what life represents. If the original design was divided into these four times, it's because each one carries a transformation needed to live perfectly balanced.

Summer represents the season of joy, the good days in which we typically make plans for vacations, family gatherings, time off, and bucket-list items. It's when we feel we have it all. We may feel beautiful, loved, successful, accomplished, and valued. This is the season we should make sure to ride out to the fullest because after the summer comes the fall.

Fall represents the season in which many things are cut off, casted, and stripped away. This is the season of change. In this time, many things will occur that have no explanation or you might not understand, but they will be necessary and crucial for you to receive what comes next. This is possibly when close people we considered friends walk away, jobs are lost, financial stability is impacted, or a health issue is diagnosed. It may seem chaotic today, but it will make sense tomorrow.

Fall can also be very beautiful with the change of colors and the decrease of the hot temperature into a more comfortable ambiance, but it also announces the winter. The fall prepares us for a season in which we will mainly be behind closed doors and alone because winter represents the season of transformation. Nothing looks or feels the same. The environment changes, the temperature in many countries decrease, and many people become the most nostalgic.

Winter strips everything away to be made new. This is the moment in life in which you might emotionally feel at your weakest and feel everything around you has been destroyed. Many people during hard times walk alone, cry alone, and have no other option but to trust that even though it doesn't make sense and it truly hurts, in the end, it will make you stronger and wiser.

The most beautiful announcement winter makes is that after all is broken down, it will all be made new. You see, right after this powerful season comes spring. Spring is the season of new beginnings in which life reemerges. Colors, movements, and nature rise again, and what was bare is now fulfilled. This is the time in which you understand the reasons behind the chaos. You begin to embrace the new that came from the old. New people are placed, doors begin to open that you never thought possible, and what you thought you couldn't overcome is now a mere past experience that helped you appreciate what you have today.

Without past failures, there wouldn't be present victories. So it doesn't matter in which season you are currently, whether you are in your best moment (summer) or currently in a season in which you feel everything is being stripped away (fall); maybe you are in a moment in life were you have lost hope and faith in believing that this will pass (winter), or you might be walking in a completely unknown time in which new people, opportunities, and emotions have developed, and you are starting over (spring); regardless of the moment you are in, be sure to celebrate the highs, be aware of the lows, and enjoy the ride.

We live by years, and those years are divided into months; the months are divided into days, the days to hours, and the hours to minutes. Even the minutes are then divided into seconds. Everything has a reason to be and a purpose. Nothing is final. Appreciate it all. If you learn to identify how this beautiful life cycle runs, you can prepare your thoughts and emotions accordingly. This will make it a lot better to manage when the unexpected events occur.

When you get on a rollercoaster ride and harness in your seat, you are fully aware that this will not be a one-direction ride. You feel ready and confident to go straight, get pulled up, get slammed down, and twist and turn along the way. You will most likely go through many emotions: the excitement of the thrill and anxiety of the rise knowing that a deep slope will follow, together with tight turns and even inversions, but in the end, you have the certainty that it will all pass, and you will be safe at the starting point once again.

A decision toward a transformation journey will be filled with the same emotions as a rollercoaster ride. Once you are seated, there is no other way of getting out but facing and living the ride. In real life, it is facing the process that will make you stronger. You will laugh, cry, and be afraid or maybe even anxious, but in the end, you will see that you made it to the other side, ready to go on the next ride that has been prepared for you. Trust and enjoy the process, it will result in the best version of yourself and make your journey a beautiful voyage toward your destiny.

VOYAGE

"Your direction is more important than your speed! Focus on your craft, stay out of the mix, and master inner peace. The treasure is really in the journey."

Now that you are aware that your transformation will be a fun-filled journey full of ups and downs, it is important to focus on the voyage that will take you there and not the speed. It's not about rushing but rather on persisting until you can achieve every goal and milestone you yearn to reach. When I meditate about this journey, I think back to the process that a caterpillar goes through before becoming a butterfly from a recent video I saw on *YouTube™* called *The Great Transformation*. In its initial stage, in which many consider the insect to be insignificant and even ugly, the caterpillar begins to prepare itself for what it knows will be a difficult but beautiful metamorphosis.

The caterpillar begins a phase in which it eats almost nonstop. It starts to create a reserve that will later be used as an adult and will have accumulated enough body mass to carry it through the entire life cycle. This is the feeding stage, and it does not stop until it is fully grown. It then moves to a more appropriate location to continue the transformation process. Once secure in the correct space, it goes into the transition stage.

In this transitional phase is when true changes occur. It may appear from the outside that nothing is happening, but inside the pupa, everything is being made new. It goes in as one creature, and after being closed out from the world and undergoing its own changes in silence, it comes out as a new animal.

Now, you might read this and think, what does this have to do with your personal voyage? Simple,

66 what you start to work on in private will later be acknowledged in public.

For others to see who you truly are, you have to be aware that, for the most part, it will require you to work hard on your own.

The first stage was the eating stage (preparation). It did not stop until it was fully prepared, fully grown. You have to work as hard as you can, focus, not give up, and maintain perseverance. Do not stop trying. Do not stop learning. Invest in yourself and keep moving forward until you start to achieve every milestone on your way to your best version. Celebrate each victory for ten minutes, and refocus and advance to your next challenge.

The second phase was composed of two things: moving to the right place to transition and becoming a new creature. Along your life, you will have to make moves and changes to advance. If you are not happy, advancing, or growing in the place you are today, it's time to move. This applies to work, friends, and relationships.

Sometimes a simple shift or change will cause an avalanche of things that were destined to come loose and manifest themselves. When you are at the right place, have the right profession, are surrounded by the right people, and are loved the right way, all the pieces fall into place. Continue to work in silence and let your results speak for themselves. In the same way the butterfly is released from its pupa, truly transformed, you can also walk in your best season. Your best days have not begun.

Never conform. Resignation is the worst enemy you can have by your side. When you stop evolving and allow frustration, defeat, and negativity to dominate your thoughts, you will fall back into bad habits, and you will most likely want to stop moving forward in your expedition. You have to believe in your capabilities and push beyond them.

I once read a quote on Instagram that said a shark in a fish tank will grow eight inches, but in the ocean, it will grow up to eight feet or bigger. The shark will never outgrow its environment, and the same is true about you. Many times, small-minded people surround us, so we don't grow. The challenge is: change your environment and watch your growth. You have to believe that you are good enough, smart enough, beautiful enough, and strong enough. Believe it and never let insecurity run your life.

The two things in life that you have complete control over are your attitude and effort. Keep in mind that you are not in a competition with anyone. Don't invest valuable time in your journey to playing the game of being better than anyone. You should simply focus on being a better person than you were yesterday. Nobody is your enemy. Your enemy is your ego, lack of focus, jealousy, procrastination, gaps in your knowledge, inability to believe you deserve more, excuses and self-doubt, and fear. That is the only enemy to focus on: yourself.

One of the affirmations that I repeat to myself every day is the following:

"My life is great. I am great. Everything is happening for me. All of the things that I am currently experiencing are only taking me to the next level of my life. I am growing. I am getting better. I choose to believe in sudden miracles and unexpected blessings."

Starting each day believing that all things are working together in your favor will change your life. This journey that you have begun will help you heal others. Never downgrade your dreams or goals just to fit your reality; upgrade your conviction to match your destiny. After all, this is what you are working for. Love yourself, know that you are beautiful, and be your best ally and fan.

There is no better representation of beauty than someone who is unafraid to be themselves and is proud of who they are. Beauty has nothing to do with looks, it has to do with your attitude and aura. You have no need for external validation.

Walk with your head up high, never look away, and be the kind of person who makes others want to step up their game. This is why you should never give up on a dream just because it will take time to accomplish it. Time will pass by anyway, and how you decide to make each day count is all on you. Success is not an accident. It is hard work, perseverance, learning, studying, sacrifice, and most of all, the love of what you are doing or learning to do.

Take advantage of the voyage you are in toward your personal growth. Remember how dwelling in your past or being anxious for the future can prevent you from enjoying your today. It is guaranteed that you will face failures and doubts along your way, but you become unstoppable when you continue on despite them.

Make certain that you spend your time on activities that are productive and take you in the direction of your goals because the person you will be in five years is based on what you do today. What you feed your mind will shape your future, so commit to feeding it with successful thoughts and surround yourself with those who have the same ambition. If you don't feed your mind with success, it will ride with mediocracy.

Learn to be cautious when it comes to the energy you let into your life. Choose places, people, and conversations wisely. In the end, they become you. So, enjoy your voyage to the best version of yourself. Remember to breathe along the way. Accept, release, and transform. If there is life, there are opportunities. I will see you on the other side!

NEW BEGINNINGS

"The secret to both mental and physical health is not to mourn about the past or worry about the future. But instead, live in the present moment."

I have completely enjoyed sharing with each of you the advice and experiences that have helped me become the person I am today. I am very hopeful that within these pages, there might be something written that could be of inspiration and will serve as the starting point of your journey toward a new season.

In my personal journey, it has not only been a matter of thinking differently. I have also had to embrace new habits and establish new routines that helped me maintain consistency.

If you work hard for a change and finally reach your goal but do not strive to maintain the results, you will end up bouncing back to your old habits and ways of thinking. It's very similar to when a person decides to lose weight and undergo a body transformation. They can work hard, follow a regimen, join a gym, and reach their goal weight, but if they don't establish a new healthy and active lifestyle and start repeating old habits, they will gain back all the weight and even more than they originally had. What they worked so hard to achieve becomes a lost cause because maintenance requires consistency.

" Transformation is not a temporary decision; it's living a new lifestyle.

You have gone through too many trials to go back. If you decide to move forward, you need to make sure that all of your following actions are calculated and predetermined to assure that you continue to grow and advance. This is why I want to share with you ten seeds of wisdom that have helped me and continue to be the foundation of my stability.

Meditation

I have made it a daily habit to meditate. One of the best definitions I have come across regarding meditation is that it offers time for relaxation and heightened awareness. It's a good practice of focused concentration, by which we experience the love, joy, peace, and stillness that is within ourselves. It is the process of experiencing God's love for ourselves by taking our attention away from the outside world. Find time to get outside and be in touch with nature. Be grateful, appreciate, give to others, and live fearlessly.

Meditation is also the highest form of prayer and intentional thinking. It's taking all of the thoughts that run through your mind and becoming aware and mindful of them but not silencing them. It is the means by which the soul expresses its love to a higher force. And as some of you may know, the body's chakras work in partnership with your life force energy, so when your chakras are in alignment, your physical and spiritual self are fully receptive to energy. This is when you will feel more at peace, become more patient, embrace solitude, and start your healing process. So why not add this beautiful routine to your life? When you can connect to what goes beyond what the natural eye can see, meditation can become your own inner retreat. Meditation is the perfect antidote for the body, mind, and soul. Try it.

Disconnect and Reconnect

At least three to four times a year, I make sure to disconnect from technology and reconnect with myself via spiritual retreats. If you have never done one, this is a perfect experience to add to your bucket list. It's literally turning off time for a moment.

During this period that you separate yourself, you can experience complete renewal and gain a high level of self-knowledge. It produces high levels of peace because you are usually surrounded by nature and away from noise and distraction. This allows you to focus only on your well-being. It is a good opportunity to connect with your spirituality, no matter what you believe in, and focus on yourself. All you need is the willingness to recenter your thoughts and your emotions.

Sometimes learning how to let go and relax can be a challenge for many people, especially those who are accustomed to always being on the run and have chaotic lifestyles or careers. Make the space to be intentional in taking time off for yourself. Vacations are great, but they don't necessarily provide the renewal that you may be seeking.

Mind Discipline

Make it a habit to exercise your mind. Many people focus on exercising the body and make it an intention to keep in shape, but they are not aware of the importance of mental fitness. It is just as important and should not be neglected. It is vital that we learn how to slow down, decompress, and boost our memory. When we go to bed at night generally the body starts to unwind and relax but the mind sometimes does not follow. It's as if you can't shut it down or turn off the thoughts. Doing things that boost mindfulness will help. Visualization is great for disconnecting and slowing down the mind as a way of destressing. Reading, daydreaming, meditation, and finding good humor in life also helps. Play games! There are now so many apps that promote and offer options that stimulate the portions of your brain that benefit from these exercises, use them. Take the time to spend a few minutes relaxing, visualizing, affirming, and doing memory exercises. The mind is a beautiful thing, be intentional in caring for it.

The Power of Manifestation

Many people do not believe in the power of manifestation or in word affirmations, but in my case, I have many testimonies of how what I have decided to manifest and affirm for my life has later become a tangible reality.

You may have heard people who have overcome emotional abuse testify that they heard so many time people tell them that they were worthless and they ended up believing this was true. They took a lie to their heart, and their minds converted it into their false truth. As a result, they were set back for many years and didn't try to strive for anything different, bigger, or better because they believed the words that were repeated to them over and over again.

If negative words and affirmations can cause someone to give up and remain still, can you imagine what positive affirmations and reinforcements can do? It can make you powerful! Every morning, part of your routine should be looking at yourself in the mirror and telling yourself how blessed you are in every part of your life. You should be thankful for health, wellness, wealth, emotional and spiritual stability, friends, family, and love. Your mind will embrace the words that your heart manifests. Be sure to nourish your mind and soul with healthy thoughts and affirmations.

Discharge and Shake Off

I have said it many times in the book, my social media, and on interviews, it is crucial that you make it a habit of continuously detoxing from people, things, and places. Every season in your life has its uniqueness. For you to not latch on to things that hold you back, you must keep in mind the reason, season, and lifetime theory. You will come across people, things, places, opportunities, and so on that are predetermined to be with you for one of these three timings. For example: you might meet a person today who has a specific reason to be in your life. Maybe they will be the bridge into a new opportunity, or they helped you solve a specific problem. Beyond this, there might not be any other reason for them to remain in your life. They served a purpose, and you may never see or interact with them ever again.

On the other hand, there are people who will be assigned to a season of your life. These are the people of whom you need to be cautious. They will be of blessing to your life during the time assigned. You will laugh and cry with them, you will learn to love and trust them, and they will have your back and even become part of your inner circle for some time. But when it comes to the moment to let them go because they are not meant to be part of your new season, on occasions, we decide to latch onto to them because we have developed emotional ties to them. We are not willing to let them go. It's not necessarily that they are bad people or that they may be intentionally hurting you; it's just a matter of personal growth.

If a relationship with a person is not adding value to your life and, quite the opposite, they serve as strongholds that don't let you move forward or advance, they are setting you back. These people were part of a specific season or period of your life, but you will have to let them go. Some may even be taken away from you, and you will never understand why.

By personal experience, I can tell you that when you progress in life and start achieving milestones, you end up repeating the example of Jesus. Hundreds surrounded him, he had an inner circle of twelve, and he did specific miracles with three, but only one stood next to him by the cross. It is most likely that the people who stand by you at the beginning of your journey will not be the same at the end.

Then there are those who come into your life for a lifetime. These are the people who value you because of your virtues but love you despite your flaws. They celebrate your milestones harder than you, know in advance what you will need when you live certain outcomes, will tell you what you need to listen versus what you want to hear, and will stand by you even if they are not publicly rewarded. These are my favorite people!

Those you don't necessarily speak to or text every day, but when you do, it's like if you never stopped talking. They know when and how to show up and will not be quick to leave.

Lifetime friendships are very valuable because you will always have a safe place to turn to in a time of need. So just as people, this same principle applies to places, things, and opportunities. Embrace your today and the people in it, but be aware that not all will remain by you every step of the way.

Decide to Be Happy

Keep a simple yet brilliant reminder that your happiness is up to you, and no one else can bring you joy or long-lasting peace of mind. When you take ownership of your happiness and become aware that no one carries that responsibility but yourself, no one can ever take it away.

Make time to eat at your favorite restaurant, laugh every day, dance like no one is watching, dress up and get beautiful for you, reward yourself, pay it forward, learn something new, read a book, appreciate art, wake up with a coffee, appreciate the stars with a wine, and repeat to yourself: *I am worthy.*

Happiness doesn't look only one way. It's important for you to truly think about what makes you happy and embrace it. This concept is different for everyone. Happiness for one person can be completely the opposite for someone else. Some people think happiness is a feeling, and others argue it's a decision; whether you believe one or the other, make sure you make choices every day that make you happy and are connected to the things that make you smile and feel safe.

People can say many things to you and about you, but you decide what affects you. You give it authority to dwell in your heart or if you brush it away. You are the owner of your thoughts, feelings, and emotions. You deserve to be happy.

Fasting and Setting Intentions

Fasting is not only a great alternative to lose and maintain weight off, but it is also a great alternative to connect with your body and soul. It is not about depriving your body from food just for weight loss; fasting will bring you clarity of thought and, when accompanied with spiritual meditation, it can be a great tool when going through a process of decision-making and creating strategies.

Life has allowed me to move from one fullness to another, expanding my mind, manifesting abundance, and broadening awareness. Setting your intentions for the things that you wish to achieve will help you get greater direction, greater focus, will increase your productivity so that you reach your goals in a shorter amount of time, and will result in higher levels of motivation.

Energy Is Everything

I made a conscious decision to become the type of energy that no matter where I go, I add value to those around me. No amount of beauty or intellect will be as valuable as a good heart and a kind human. I know I am a powerful, manifesting queen, and I welcome financial, spiritual, and physical stability in my life, and that is the type of energy I want to put out in the universe. My wish is that when I enter a room, people are touched, and the atmosphere is transformed.

If you have studied the matter, or if you do a research on the web you will learn for example on the Learn Religions website that to energy medicine practitioners, there are five fields of human energy: physical, etheric, emotional, mental, and spiritual. The physical layer is the layer most perceived and the only one that can be touched and seen, but as you study the different layers, you will find the etheric field, followed by the emotional layer. This is where our feelings and fears reside. The fourth layer is the mental energy or field. This is the layer from where our ideas and belief systems are stored. Our thoughts get sorted here, and this is where we keep our personal truths.

The deepest field is the spiritual energy. The spiritual layer of the human energy is the place where our high awareness resides. This layer ties us to our past lives and universal consciousness. There is so much to you that you might not be aware of it. This is why connecting to other people's energy is so powerful. When you are conscious of this and are intentional of putting out good energy, you will always add value to the people around you.

Be Better, Every Day

A beautiful day begins with a beautiful mindset; that is why my goal every day is to become a better human being. Something that is really hard but at the same time truly amazing is giving up on being perfect and beginning the work of being yourself. As mentioned before, you are not in competition with anyone else but yourself. When you measure yourself against your past results or experiences and try to exceed them, you end up with a better version of yourself every day.

Perfection does not exist. Some people believe that "being a perfectionist" is a good quality, but sometimes it works against you. When you carry the pressure of wanting everything to be perfect and feel the need to constantly measure up, you will refrain yourself from trying new things or be open to new opportunities based on the fear of failing or not doing it perfectly.

Failure is part of success. You don't need to be perfect; you need to give excellence. Excellence and perfection are not the same. If you work on being better every day, there are no limits on how far you can progress. You are your biggest threat and cheerleader. Be your best fan! Do not let your potential go to waste.

Like I have said time and time again: new goals don't deliver new results; new lifestyles do, and a lifestyle is not an outcome; it's a process. For this reason, your energy shouldn't go to chasing better results but instead to building better habits.

Gratitude Journal

Finally, one final seed I can share with you is keep a gratitude journal. If you make it a practice to write down a minimum of three to five things that you are grateful for at the end of the day, you will soon realize it's more the things you have than the things you lack. If you concentrate on what you have, you will always end up having and achieving more. On the other hand, if your primary focus is on what you don't have or what has not yet arrived, you will never feal satisfied. You will constantly feel there is a void in your life.

Many successful and famous people keep a gratitude journal and testify that when you make it a habit, the spiritual dimensions in your life begin to change; it opens up and expands, and you end up growing.

Every day is a gift and new opportunity. Learn to love the little miracles you see each day. When you start noticing them, you will realize that there are always good things happening all around you, even if they are not directly tied to you.

The smallest seed can produce the biggest fruit. That is the beauty behind such a miraculous process. When you plant a seed, you don't see the result of what will develop and rise immediately. It is a silent process that takes place under the surface where no eyes can see. It isn't until the seed dies to its original design that what it carries transforms into something completely different and new. When the time is right and the conditions are correct, the end result is manifested.

Work hard and do it in silence. Let your transformation speak for itself. Let your growth and success be what people see when the time and conditions are right. I am not sharing something with you that I have not applied to myself. I learned along my journey that my dreams are not to be shared with everyone, my weaknesses should not be told to all ears, and my biggest and strongest ally is my determination. I am blessed to know that I could be of inspiration in your journey. Remember: *"The secret to both mental and physical health is not to mourn about the past or worry about the future. **But instead, live in the present moment.**"*

CPSIA information can be obtained
at www.ICGtesting.com
Printed in the USA
BVHW031443020822
643612BV00013B/1396

9 798218 032777